AF262818

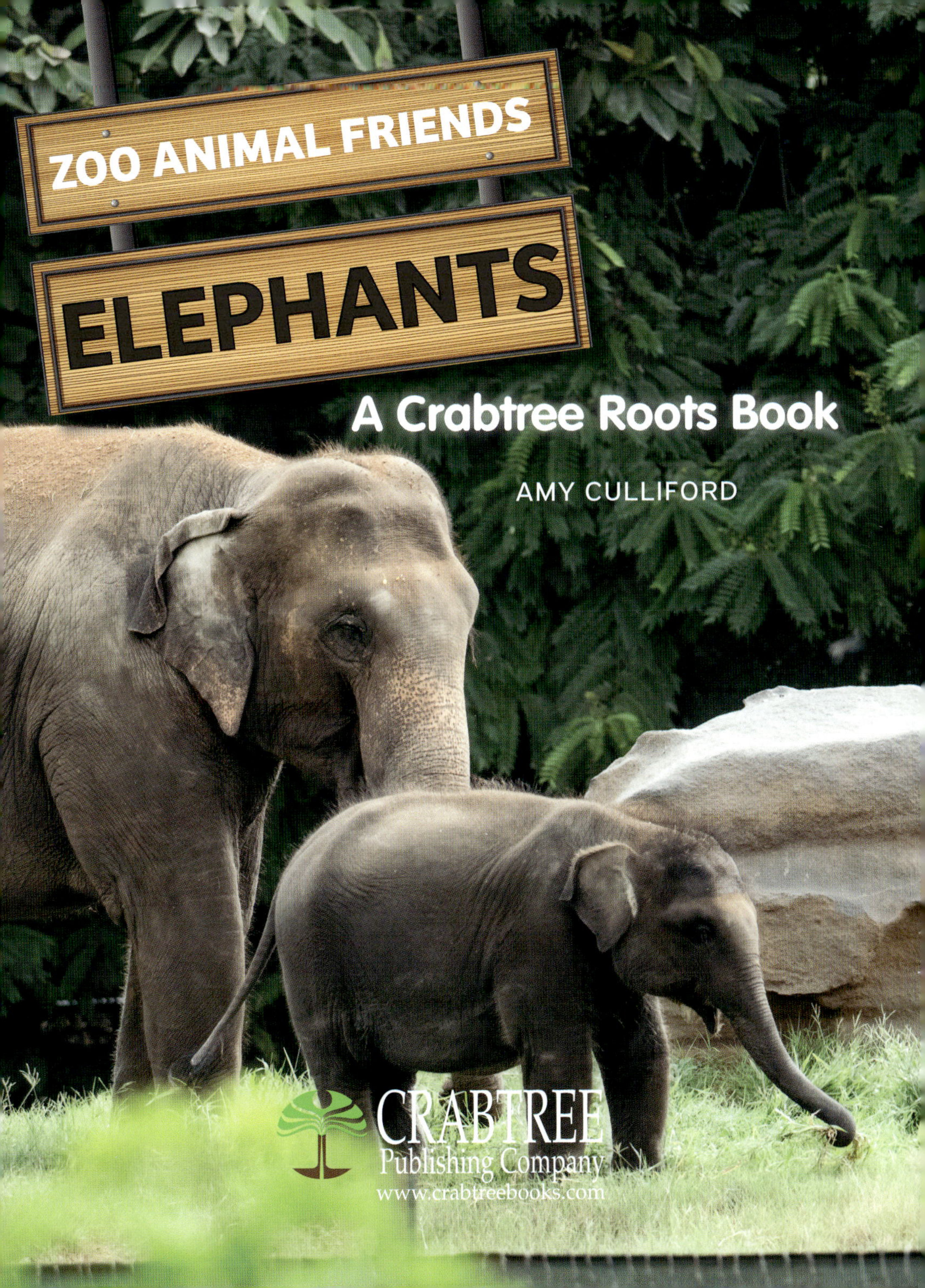

ZOO ANIMAL FRIENDS
ELEPHANTS
A Crabtree Roots Book
AMY CULLIFORD
CRABTREE
Publishing Company
www.crabtreebooks.com

School-to-Home Support for Caregivers and Teachers

This book helps children grow by letting them practice reading. Here are a few guiding questions to help the reader with building his or her comprehension skills. Possible answers appear here in red.

Before Reading:

- What do I think this book is about?
  - *I think this book is about elephants.*
  - *I think this book is about where elephants live.*

- What do I want to learn about this topic?
  - *I want to learn more about baby elephants.*
  - *I want to learn more about the friends elephants have.*

During Reading:

- I wonder why...
  - *I wonder why elephants are so big.*
  - *I wonder why elephants have such big ears.*

- What have I learned so far?
  - *I have learned that elephants have long trunks.*
  - *I have learned that elephants like to play in water.*

After Reading:

- What details did I learn about this topic?
  - *I have learned that elephants like to eat.*
  - *I have learned that most elephants are gray.*

- Read the book again and look for the vocabulary words.
  - *I see the word **trunks** on page 6 and the word **gray** on page 9. The other vocabulary words are found on page 14.*

This is an **elephant**.

All elephants are big!

Many elephants have long **trunks**.

Most elephants
are **gray**.

Elephants like to play in water.

All elephants like
to eat.

Word List

Sight Words

all	in	play
an	is	this
are	like	to
big	long	water
eat	many	
have	most	

Words to Know

elephant

gray

trunks

28 Words

This is an **elephant**.

All elephants are big!

Many elephants have long **trunks**.

Most elephants are **gray**.

Elephants like to play in water.

All elephants like to eat.

Written by: Amy Culliford
Designed by: Rhea Wallace
Series Development : James Earley
Proofreader: Petrice Custance
Educational Consultant: Marie Lemke M.Ed.

Photographs:
Shutterstock: Tatiana Litvinova: cover; P.V.R. Murty:
    p. 1; Mary Prentice: p. 3; Erika Kusuma Wardani: p.
    5; Santod32: p. 7; meunierd: p. 8; Steve Wilson: p.
    11; hangingpixels: p. 12-13

Library and Archives Canada Cataloguing in Publication

CIP available at Library and Archives Canada

Library of Congress Cataloging-in-Publication Data

CIP available at Library of Congress

Crabtree Publishing Company

www.crabtreebooks.com   1-800-387-7650

Published in the United States
Crabtree Publishing
347 Fifth Avenue, Suite 1402-145
New York, NY, 10016

Published in Canada
Crabtree Publishing
616 Welland Ave.
St. Catharines, ON, L2M 5V6